D1357294

C334321848

THE
SHANG
DYNASTY

Tim Cooke

W
FRANKLIN WATTS
LONDON • SYDNEY

Published in Great Britain in 2018 by
The Watts Publishing Group

For Brown Bear Books Ltd:
Managing Editor: Tim Cooke
Children's Publisher: Anne O'Daly
Editorial Director: Lindsey Lowe
Design Manager: Keith Davis
Designer and Illustrator: Supriya Sahai
Picture Manager: Sophie Mortimer

Concept development: Square and Circus/
Brown Bear Books Ltd

ISBN: 978 1 4451 6191 4

Printed in Malaysia

Franklin Watts
An imprint of
Hachette Children's Group
Part of the Watts Publishing Group
Carmelite House
50 Victoria Embankment
London EC4Y 0DZ

An Hachette UK company
www.hachette.co.uk
www.franklinwatts.co.uk

FSC
www.fsc.org
MIX
Paper from
responsible sources
FSC® C137506

CONTENTS

THE SHANG DYNASTY

The Shang ruled China from about 1600 to 1046 BCE. The reign was a period of stability during which many important parts of Chinese culture first appeared. Many historians count the Shang as the first Chinese dynasty.

SHANG HISTORY

The Shang kingdom was established by Cheng Tang in the Yellow River valley, where farmers grew enough crops to support the growth of towns. The Shang enlarged their territory by defeating their neighbours, until they controlled much of eastern China. The high point of Shang rule came under King Wu Ding (ruled c.1238–1180 BCE). He built a new capital at Yin (now Anyang).

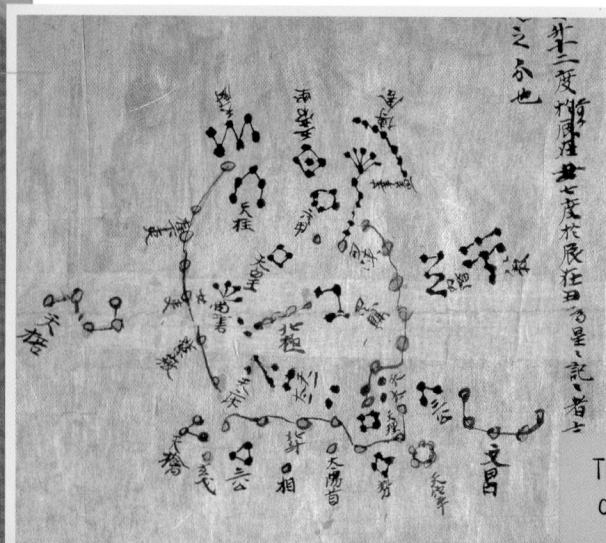

The Shang created China's first writing system. They also studied the stars to establish an accurate calendar. They introduced practices that became central to Chinese religion, such as telling the future, or divination.

This Chinese star chart was part of a long tradition of mapping the stars begun by Shang astronomers.

CHINA

MONGOLIA

CHINA

Yin
(Anyang)

SHANG
DYNASTY

INDIA

Pacific Ocean

ARTEFACTS

The Shang were skilled builders, craftspeople and artists, and some of the objects they made survive today. Those objects include bronze vessels, pieces of jade and possessions buried with dead rulers. One of the best ways to discover how the ancient Chinese lived and how they thought is by studying these artefacts. These objects allow us to step back into the world of the people who made them.

The Shang built one of the earliest versions of the Great Wall of China to protect their northern border.

FERTILE LAND

The Shang dynasty emerged in the valley of the Yellow River. The river's frequent floods carried fertile mud over the land. Shang peasants used stone tools to prepare the soil. They grew crops to support the growing population.

CHINA

Yin

Yellow River

Yangtze River

☞ THE FACTS

Under the Shang, all the land in the kingdom belonged to the king. The large population of peasants worked for the royal farms. The workers were organized into gangs to sow and harvest crops. Although later Chinese farmers learned to grow rice in wet paddy fields, the main crop of Shang farmers was millet. They grew enough grain to be able to supply food for the people who lived in towns, where they worked as craftspeople or traders.

Farmers lived in villages among their fields. They built terraces on the side of hills to provide more flat land for growing crops.

MILLET

Shang farmers grew a range of crops. The most important was millet, but they also grew barley, rice and wheat.

The farmers used stone sickles to harvest the crops. When the grain was gathered, it was taken to royal storehouses. From there, it was distributed evenly to all members of the population. Millet was ground into flour or boiled to make a porridge, called congee. It was also used to make an alcoholic drink. Only the wealthy could afford to eat fish and meat regularly.

Fertile Soil The Shang, like the Xia before them, based themselves along the Yellow River. The soil there was good for agriculture.

Millet was the main crop. It grew quickly and produced a large amount of grain.

SHANG SOCIETY

The first Shang king was Cheng Tang. He was said to have defeated the Xia in around 1600 BCE. The Xia army turned against their king because of his harsh rule. Cheng Tang made sure that Shang society was fairer and more inclusive.

Rural Society Most of the Shang lived in villages and small towns scattered in the countryside. Cheng Tang organised society to bring everyone under the protection of the king.

☞ THE FACTS

- Cheng Tang was careful to treat his subjects well. He was followed by eight more Shang kings who kept the empire stable and prosperous.
- From c.1562 to c.1401 BCE, the kingdom was weakened by fighting among the royal family before King Pan Geng restored order.
- The longest-reigning Shang king, Wu Ding, followed the principles of Cheng Tang.
- The Shang capital moved around over the history of the dynasty.

SCROLL PAINTING

This scroll painting of Cheng
Tang was painted by Ma Lin
in the early 1300s CE.

By then, Cheng Tang was
remembered as an ideal
emperor. He had established
a social system with the king
at the top, followed by other
members of the royal family.
Beneath them came the
king's nobles and advisors,
who had specialised roles
as bureaucrats, priests or
generals. They were
followed by merchants
and craftspeople. Peasant
farmers formed the largest
part of the population.
At the lowest level of
society were slaves, who
made up five per cent of
the Shang population.

湯

順天應人　本乎仁義
以質繼忠　匪曰求與
盤銘一德　桑林六事
人紀肇修　垂千萬世

Over a thousand years after
Cheng Tang's death, an artist
painted this image celebrating
his wisdom and fairness.

BRONZE

The Shang were expert craftspeople. Metalworkers made the first bronze in China by mixing copper and tin. They used moulds to make tools and weapons and to cast complex bronze objects. These objects were bought by wealthy members of society or were used in religious rituals.

Ancient metalworking techniques are still used in China.

☞ THE FACTS

- Bronze was harder wearing than previous metals had been. Bronze weapons gave Shang armies an advantage over enemies who did not use bronze, as their blades stayed sharper for longer.
- Shang craftsmen made bronze daggers, axes and arrowheads. They also made bronze helmets for protection.
- Bronze was so valuable that rulers were often buried with bronze artefacts.
- Ordinary people had tools of stone or wood, because bronze was expensive.

Bronze is made from a mixture of about 20 per cent tin and 80 per cent copper. Increasing the amount of copper makes the bronze stronger.

This is a bronze vessel from the late Shang period. It has the face of an evil spirit called a taotie, with its eyes at the top.

Bronze was usually poured into moulds to make casts. However, it could also be made in lumps and then hammered into shape by a blacksmith.

METAL CASTING

Shang metalworkers used a technique known as casting in order to create elaborate shapes.

They made a model of the object and covered it in a layer of soft clay. When the clay had dried, the craftsmen cut it from the model. This created a hollow clay mould. The workers heated bronze until it was molten, then poured it into the mould and left it to set. If needed, they used molten bronze to join sections of the object together. The moulds were then reused to make more casts.

RELIGION

The Shang introduced many ideas that remained important in Chinese religion for centuries. They worshipped their ancestors and used a technique called divination to foretell the future. The king and his priests carried out divination rituals.

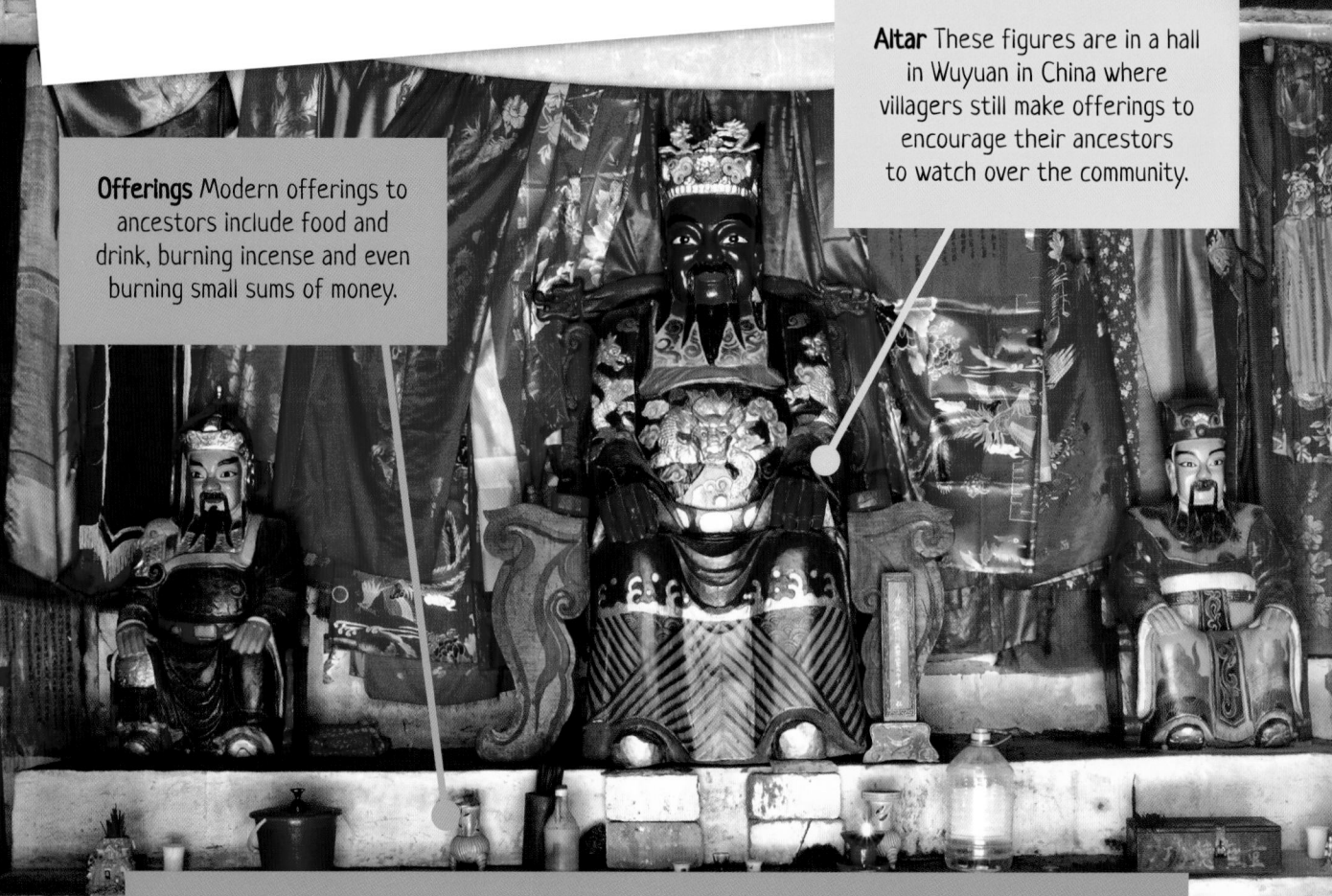

Altar These figures are in a hall in Wuyuan in China where villagers still make offerings to encourage their ancestors to watch over the community.

Offerings Modern offerings to ancestors include food and drink, burning incense and even burning small sums of money.

☞ THE FACTS

The Shang believed that people who had died continued to help living members of their family. The living offered sacrifices to make sure the spirits of the ancestors were happy. People offered food to the dead.

They sacrificed animals or even humans to them. In later Chinese religion, the ancestors remained an important object of worship. Ancestor worship continues in parts of China today.

ORACLE BONES

The Shang worshipped gods who controlled the aspects of the world that affected farmers: the Sun, Moon, wind and rain.

The chief god, Shang Di, ruled over these other deities. He gave the Shang advice on important subjects, such as when to plant crops. The king or his priests wrote questions for the god on turtle shells or cattle bones. These oracle bones were heated until they cracked. A priest called a diviner interpreted the pattern of cracks in the bone to learn Shang Di's answer to the question.

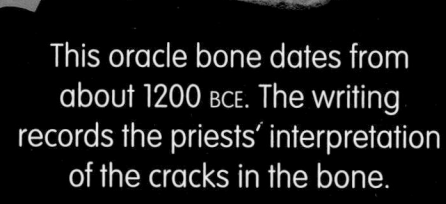

This oracle bone dates from about 1200 BCE. The writing records the priests' interpretation of the cracks in the bone.

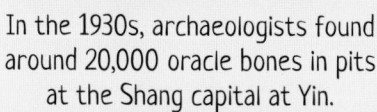

In the 1930s, archaeologists found around 20,000 oracle bones in pits at the Shang capital at Yin.

WARFARE

The Shang created their empire through the strength of their army. The conquest began when Cheng Tang overthrew the Xia, as well as the Di and Qiang peoples to the west. The Shang had the largest army in the region.

☞ THE FACTS

Shang rulers personally led their armies into battle against rival peoples, whom they gave the collective name of Fang. The Shang sometimes got on with groups of Fang, but at other times fought against them. One of the most remarkable Shang warriors was Lady Hao, a queen of Emperor Wu Ding. She went into battle at the head of a huge army of 13,000 men.

BATTLE AXE

Bronze weapons such as this battle axe gave the Shang an advantage over their enemies.

Bronze blades and arrowheads remained sharper for longer than weapons made from softer metals or wood. The Shang army included separate companies of infantry and archers. The infantry used battle axes and spears in close-quarter fighting. The archers used bows made from wood, bone and horn. Arrows from the bows could kill an enemy at a range of 180 metres. Such weapons helped make the Shang the most powerful fighting force in China.

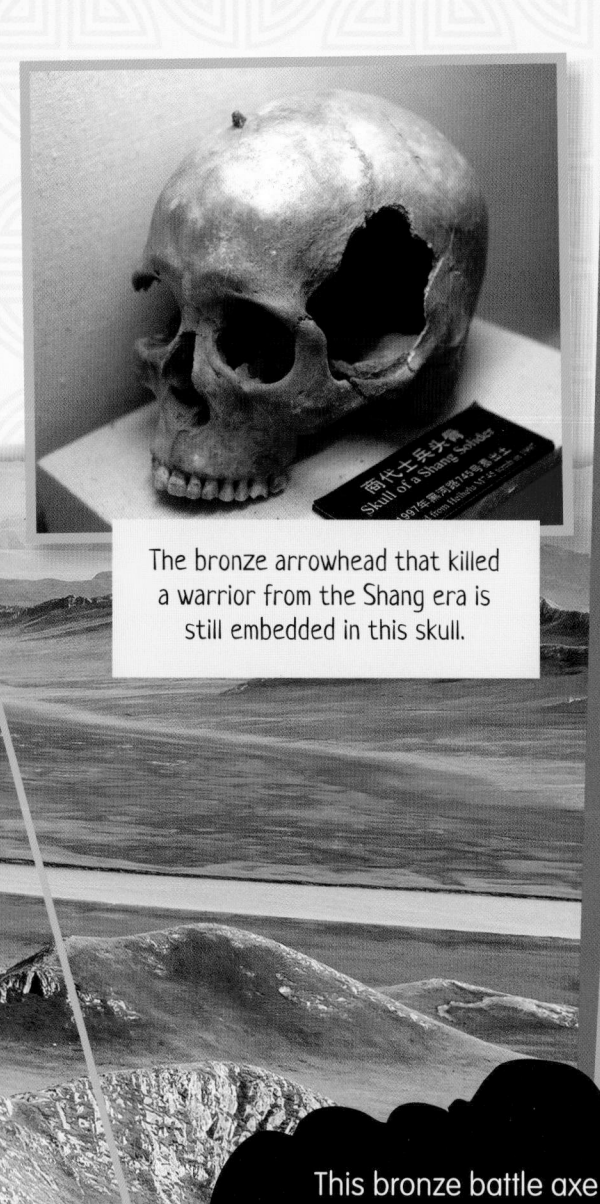

The bronze arrowhead that killed a warrior from the Shang era is still embedded in this skull.

This bronze battle axe was decorated with the face of a demon, or taotie.

Shang territory was protected from invasion by the mountains that lined the valley of the Yellow River.

DRAGONS

Dragons have been an important symbol in China ever since the Shang dynasty. Unlike in the West, the Chinese see dragons as positive creatures. Dragons are strong and vigorous, so they became the symbol of the Chinese emperor.

Dragons like this often appeared on the roofs of buildings to protect the buildings and their occupants.

☞ THE FACTS

- The first depictions of dragons in China were statues carved up to 5,000 years ago.
- Chinese dragons are usually long, thin snakelike creatures with four legs.
- Dragons featured widely in Shang art.
- The Shang believed that dragons spend their time high in the sky in summer and deep beneath the oceans in winter.
- They thought that dragons sometimes visited the land to help humans.

JADE DRAGON

Shang craftsmen depicted coiled dragons in bronze or in jade.

This jade dragon was among the treasures found in the tomb of Lady Hao in 1976. Jade was prized for its green colour and because it did not wear out. This made it a symbol of immortal life. However, the stone's hardness made it difficult to carve. Even bronze tools could not cut jade. Instead, craftsmen shaped the stone by grinding it with wet sand. The process was time-consuming, so jade was very expensive.

This carved jade dragon was found in the tomb of Lady Hao, which was discovered at Yin (Anyang) in 1976.

Most buildings had four-clawed dragons. Only imperial buildings had dragons with five claws.

This dragon is woven in silk on the robes of a Chinese emperor.

SILK

Silk was being made in China before the Shang, but the Shang probably perfected the best way to make it. Silk production is expensive, so the cloth was only used by the royal family and nobility.

This silk robe carries images of the phoenix, a legendary bird said to be able to renew itself.

☞ THE FACTS

Silk was highly prized because it was light, smooth and comfortable to wear. It was also easy to dye in bright colours. The Shang used it to make robes and also to make an early form of paper to write on. No silk survives from the Shang period because it is so delicate. In later periods of Chinese history, only members of the royal family were allowed to wear silk.

This theatrical costume was worn by a performer playing a princess in nineteenth-century entertainments at the Qing court.

Loom Lady Hsi-Ling-Shih, wife of the Yellow Emperor, China's legendary founder, is said to have invented the silk loom in about 3000 BCE.

The caterpillars of the silk moth feed on mulberry leaves before they spin their cocoons.

At times when silk was worn more widely, one important use was in theatrical costumes. The bold colours highlighted the wearer's movements.

COCOON

Silk production is very labour intensive.

The yarn is made from cocoons produced by the larvae of the silk moth. When the cocoons are ready, they are steamed to kill the larvae inside. The cocoons are then boiled in water to loosen their fine fibres, which are unravelled by hand. Five or six fibres are combined to form a thread of silk. The threads are then dyed and woven into fabric on a loom. It takes up to two thousand cocoons to make just 500 grams of silk.

TRADE

The political stability that marked most of the Shang period allowed trade to develop. Merchants could travel safely through the land, selling the creations of the best craftspeople. Shang merchants usually avoided trading with foreigners, so few goods were imported or exported.

CHINA
Yin
Yellow River
Yangtze River

👉 THE FACTS

The main trade routes followed the Yellow and Yangtze Rivers, and were usually centred on the Shang capital of the time. The royal family were the wealthiest members of society, and valuable trade goods included bronze goods that were buried in royal tombs, together with bronze weapons and musical instruments. Jade and silk were also traded, while wood and rice were brought from the south.

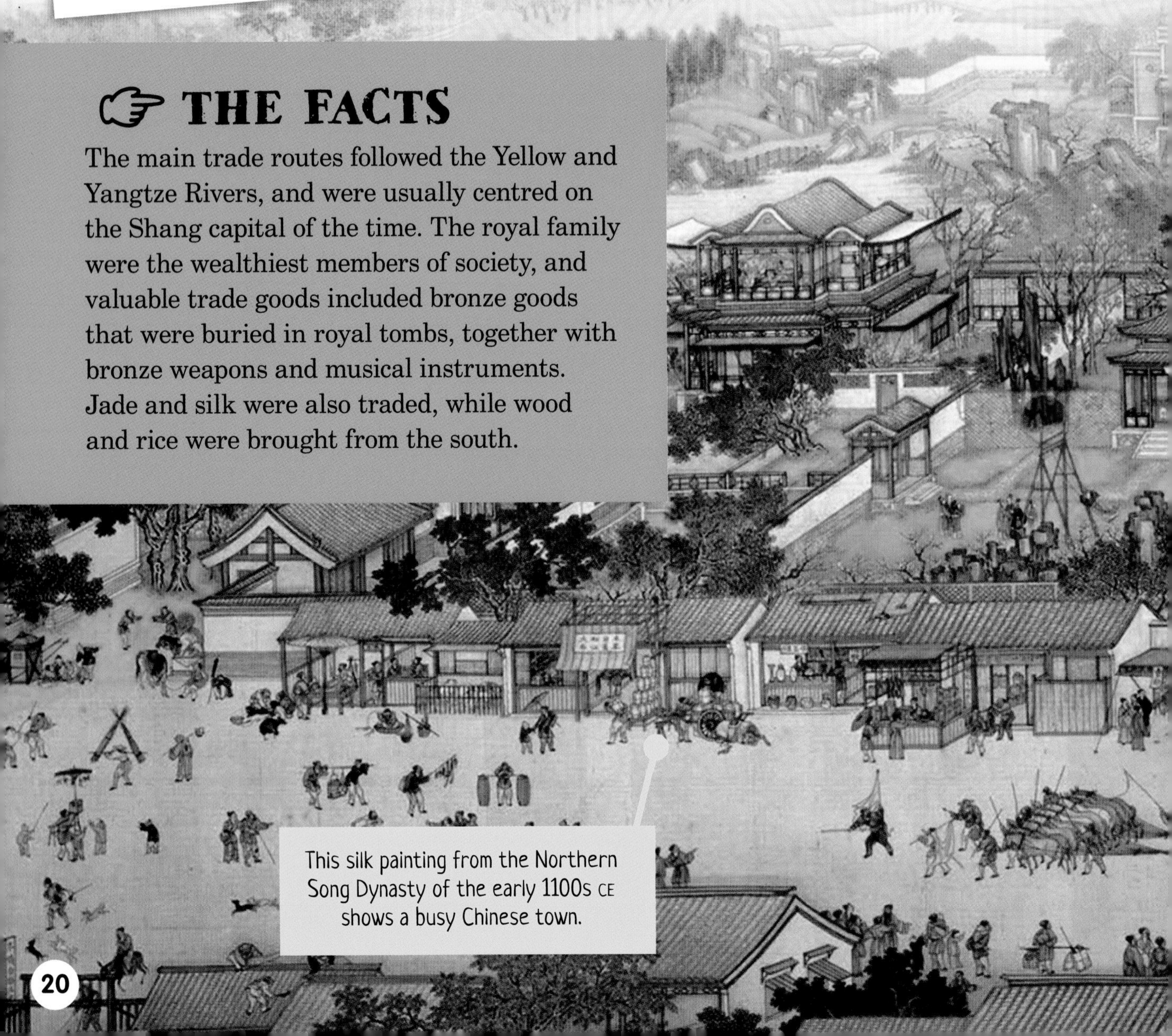

This silk painting from the Northern Song Dynasty of the early 1100s CE shows a busy Chinese town.

COWRIE SHELLS

These shells come from the money cowrie – a type of sea snail.

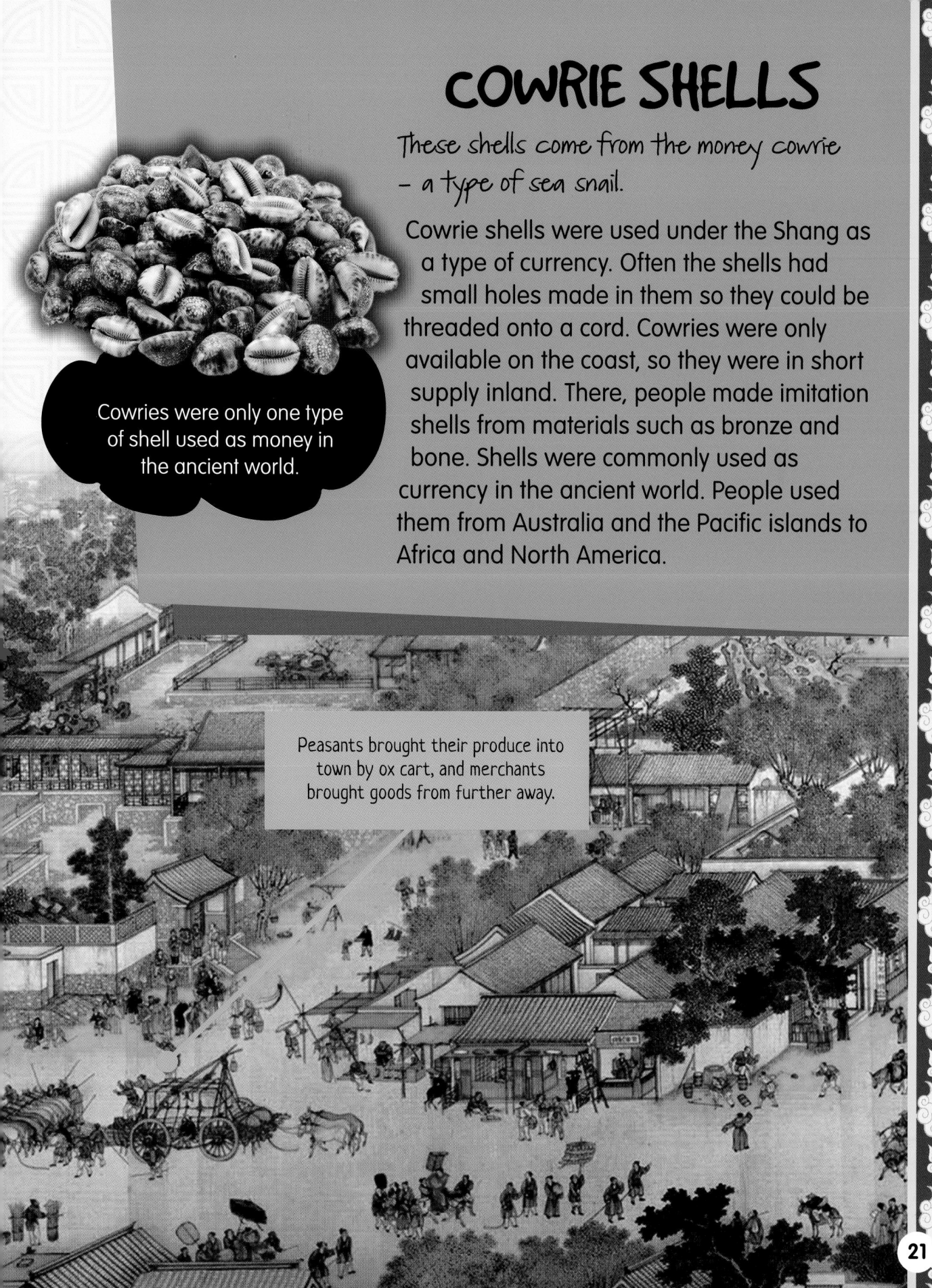

Cowrie shells were used under the Shang as a type of currency. Often the shells had small holes made in them so they could be threaded onto a cord. Cowries were only available on the coast, so they were in short supply inland. There, people made imitation shells from materials such as bronze and bone. Shells were commonly used as currency in the ancient world. People used them from Australia and the Pacific islands to Africa and North America.

Cowries were only one type of shell used as money in the ancient world.

Peasants brought their produce into town by ox cart, and merchants brought goods from further away.

WRITING

The Shang created the first Chinese writing system. Only inscriptions on oracle bones or bronze objects survive today. However, the characters the Shang invented became the basis of modern Chinese writing. Calligraphy, or beautiful writing, is still an important art form in China.

Many Chinese characters are based on what were essentially drawings of the objects they represented.

☞ THE FACTS

- The Shang writing system combined characters, which stand for sounds, and pictograms, which represent objects or abstract ideas.
- Under the Qin dynasty, from 221 to 206 BCE, the Shang characters became fixed as the basis of Chinese writing.
- Modern Chinese writing is still closely based on the Shang symbols.
- Because Chinese includes pictograms, it has far more characters than scripts that use an alphabet – around 50,000.
- Educated Chinese people today learn between three thousand and four thousand characters.

Chinese calligraphers often use brushes to paint characters to achieve different widths of line.

A calligrapher's equipment, including brushes, pens and stones for grinding pigment to make ink.

BAMBOO BOOK

This is a modern version of an early Chinese 'book'.

The Shang wrote vertically on strips of silk or bamboo. The strips were tied together so that they could be rolled up for storage or unrolled to read. The Shang wrote down the records of the empire, plus ideas about divination. Those ideas later formed the basis of the *I-Ching,* a famous book about fortune telling. However, Shang books were made of delicate materials that have rotted away over the last 3,500 years.

This modern scroll is made from strips of bamboo that have been tied together.

GRAVE GOODS

The Shang believed that the Afterlife was similar to life in this world. Rulers and nobles were buried with whatever they might need for the Afterworld. This included anything from vessels for cooking to servants who were sacrificed in order to prepare food.

CHINA

Yin

Lady Hao was buried with a roomful of precious objects, including large bronze vessels.

☞ THE FACTS

- Shang rulers were buried with objects made from valuable bronze and jade. Other grave goods included oracle bones and cowrie shells.
- Slaves were used to dig tombs up to 12 metres deep in the ground.

- The tombs of wealthy people were divided into chambers by wooden walls.
- Thirteen royal tombs have been discovered at the Shang capital at Yin (Anyang).

Lady Hao's tomb included the skeletons of sixteen servants who were buried with her.

BURIED CHARIOT

One of the most elaborate Shang tombs belonged to Lady Hao.

The queen was buried with 468 bronze objects and 755 pieces of jade, together with more than 6,000 cowrie shells. The tomb also included a number of chariots, which the Shang started using in around 1200 BCE. Their presence in the tomb reflected Lady Hao's role as a military commander.

Chariots were sometimes buried with horses to pull them and a charioteer.

YU TAMES THE FLOOD

Just as artefacts tell us a lot about cultures from the past, the stories people told reveal what they thought about their world. Most ancient cultures used myths to explain their beliefs. This story tells how Yu protected the land from floods.

A silk painting of Yu the Great from the 1200s.

In the distant past, the god Tiandi grew tired of humans' wicked behaviour. He ordered Gonggong, the god of water, to send a great flood to cover the earth and drown the people. The Emperor Yao, who ruled China then, appealed for divine help. His prayer was heard by the god Gun, who wanted to help the people.

Gun travelled through China, but could not see how to stop the floods. Then he met with an owl and a tortoise. They told him about some magic clay that swelled when it came into contact with water. The animals urged Gun to use the clay to build a dam. Gun stole enough clay from the beings who guarded it to build a giant dam. Soon the waters began to disappear from the land.

When Tiandi saw what Gun had done, he was furious.
He sent a god to kill Gun and destroy the dam.
The floodwaters rose back over the land.

Gun still wanted to help the people. From his body, he created
his son, Yu. Yu was a god who could take the shape of a
dragon. He carried on his father's work. For thirteen years,
he travelled through the kingdom, plugging the 233,599
springs from which the floodwater came. He mapped the
boundaries of the nine provinces of China. Even when he
passed his own house, he did not enter but kept travelling.

Yu took the form of a dragon and used his tail to gouge out
deep furrows in the earth. These became the valleys of China's
great rivers, which carried the floodwaters away to the sea.
Yu showed people how to use the magic clay to build dams
and dykes. In that way, he showed the Chinese how they
could protect themselves and their land.

TIMELINE OF THE SHANG DYNASTY

1562 BCE
The tenth Shang emperor, Zhong Ding, comes to the throne; he rules until 1550 BCE. Zhong Ding moves the capital from Bo to Ao, in present-day Henan Province.

c.1401 BCE
King Pan Geng comes to the throne around this time. He restores stability to the Shang after a period of turmoil and moves the Shang capital from Ao to Yin (Anyang).

c.1238 BCE
Around this time, Wu Ding becomes the twenty-second Shang king, and one of the greatest. His 58-year reign is the longest of any Shang ruler.

1600s BCE   **1500s BCE**   **1300s BCE**   **1250s BCE**

c.1600 BCE
The Shang defeat the Xia in the Battle of Mingtiao and take control of the Yellow River region. Cheng Tang becomes the first king of the Shang dynasty.

c.1250 BCE
The earliest known written Chinese records, recorded on oracle bones, date from around this time.

c.1200 BCE
The chariot is introduced to the Shang by nomadic peoples from the west.

c.1122 BCE
The Zhou dynasty is founded on the edge of the Shang empire.

1050 BCE
King Wen of Zhou dies before he can launch an attack on the Shang.

1200s BCE

1100s BCE

1000s BCE

c.1200 BCE
Lady Fu Hao, a queen of Wu Ding, is buried in a tomb full of personal possessions.

c.1075 BCE
Xi Din becomes the last Shang ruler.

1046 BCE
The Zhou overthrow the last Shang king, Di Xin in the Battle of Muye.

1049 BCE
Wu succeeds his father as king of the Zhou.

GLOSSARY

archaeologists people who use old objects and buildings to study the past

artefacts objects that have been made by people

astronomers people who study the stars and planets in the sky

bureaucrats officials who help keep records in the government

chariots open horse-drawn vehicles with two wheels, usually used for warfare

deities supernatural beings, such as gods and goddesses

divination predicting the future through supernatural means

dynasty a sequence of rulers who are all related to one another

fertile full of nutrients for growing plants

immortal living for ever

imperial relating to an empire or emperor

inclusive containing everyone

infantry soldiers who fight on foot

jade a hard green stone used for ornaments and jewellery

larvae caterpillars or grubs that form a young stage in the lives of butterflies and moths

fertile having the ability to grow plants easily

nobles people who belonged to the elite class of society

oracle bones animal bones used for divination by heating them and studying the pattern of cracks

paddy fields fields that are deliberately flooded with shallow water in order to grow rice

peasants poor agricultural workers who do not own their own land

pictograms written characters that are based on pictures

Qing A dynasty that ruled China from 1644 to 1912

rituals religious ceremonies consisting of a series of actions

sacrifices valuable things given to gods as offerings, often in the form of food or drink

sickles short-handled tools with curved blades for harvesting crops and grasses

terraces flat steps dug into a hillside

FURTHER RESOURCES

Books

The Chinese Empire, Ellis Roxburgh
(Wayland, 2017)

Ancient China, Izzi Howell
(Wayland, 2016)

Shang Dynasty China, Tracey Kelly
(Franklin Watts, 2016)

The Shang Dynasty of Ancient China, Geoffrey Barker
(Wayland, 2015)

The Shang Dynasty, Alex Woolf
(Badger Publishing, 2015)

Websites

www.bbc.co.uk/education/clips/zcsxv4j
This BBC site has a short video about the Shang Dynasty.

www.bbc.co.uk/education/clips/zsgj4j6
This BBC site has a short video about how the Shang invented
Chinese writing.

**www.bbc.co.uk/programmes/articles/
4cYrml3Tpf7hDW4PDzzgCRg/chinas-bronze-age**
A BBC page that investigates a number of Shang artefacts.

learnodo-newtonic.com/shang-dynasty-facts
Ten fascinating facts about the Shang dynasty.

www.theschoolrun.com/homework-help/shang-dynasty
These pages about ancient China are intended to help students
with study projects.

INDEX

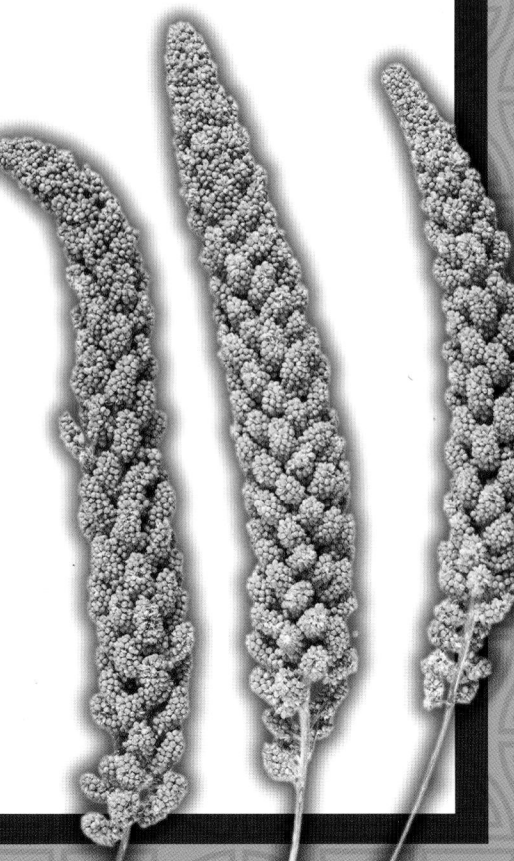